Pepperoni Pizza Cookbook

A Delectable Collection of Pepperoni Infused Pizza Recipes for Every Occasion

While every precaution has been taken in the preparation of this book, the publisher assumes no responsibility for errors or omissions, or for damages resulting from the use of the information contained herein.

PEPPERONI PIZZA COOKBOOK

First edition. January 27, 2024.

ISBN: 979-8224444427

Written by john ahmad.

Table of Contents

John Ahmad

Chapter 1: The Art of Pepperoni: A Journey into Flavor

Pepperoni, with its distinctive smoky aroma and bold flavors, has long been a beloved topping in the world of pizza. Its spicy kick and mouthwatering appeal have made it a staple for pizza enthusiasts everywhere. In this chapter, we'll take a deep dive into the world of pepperoni, exploring its origins, the processes that create its iconic taste, and how it has become an integral part of pizza culture.

The Origins of Pepperoni on Pizza

Pepperoni's journey as a pizza topping has an interesting history. While it's commonly associated with Italian cuisine, its roots can be traced back to the United States, where it evolved from the term "peperoni," which originally referred to bell peppers. The term underwent a transformation in the United States to represent the spicy, cured sausage we know today. It was the merging of Italian-American culinary traditions with a touch of spice that led to the birth of pepperoni as a pizza topping. Its popularity soared, and it quickly became a standard choice for pizza lovers seeking a burst of heat and flavor.

The Making of Pepperoni

The process of crafting pepperoni is an art in itself. Traditional pepperoni is made from a mixture of finely ground beef and pork. This mixture is seasoned with a carefully balanced blend of spices, including paprika, red pepper flakes, black pepper, garlic, and fennel seeds. These spices contribute to the characteristic smokiness and spiciness that define pepperoni's flavor profile. Once the meat is seasoned, it's stuffed into casings, usually made from natural or synthetic materials, and then cured to develop its distinct taste. The curing process not only preserves the meat but also infuses it with a smoky depth that complements the spices, resulting in the signature pepperoni flavor.

The Evolution of Pepperoni Varieties

While the classic beef and pork pepperoni remains a favorite, variations have emerged over the years to cater to diverse dietary preferences. For those seeking a leaner option, turkey pepperoni has gained popularity. Made from turkey meat, it offers a lighter alternative that doesn't compromise on the spiciness and flavor associated with pepperoni. Moreover, the demand for plant-based options has led to the creation of vegan and vegetarian pepperoni alternatives, allowing individuals with different dietary choices to enjoy the classic taste.

The Perfect Pepperoni Slice

Achieving the perfect pepperoni slice is a delicate art. When baked, the pepperoni should curl slightly at the edges, forming those irresistible crispy cups that trap flavor and hold a touch of oil—adding an extra layer of indulgence. The heat also releases the oils and spices in the pepperoni, infusing the entire pizza with its distinctive aroma. This tantalizing aroma, often likened to the warmth of a pizzeria, is a significant part of the pizza experience, heightening anticipation as you take that first bite.

Pairing Pepperoni with Other Ingredients

Pepperoni's robust flavor profile makes it a versatile companion for a wide range of pizza toppings. Its spiciness can be balanced by the richness of cheeses like mozzarella and cheddar. Tangy ingredients like olives, pickled peppers, and banana peppers provide a contrast that elevates the overall taste.

For those who enjoy a hint of sweetness, pineapple can add a delightful and unexpected twist. Combining pepperoni with vegetables such as mushrooms, onions, and bell peppers offers a balance between the savory notes of the meat and the freshness of the produce.

Pepperoni is more than just a pizza topping; it's a journey into flavor. Its rich history, intricate crafting process, and diverse variations have cemented its place in culinary culture. Whether you're a fan of the classic combination or eager to explore new frontiers of taste, pepperoni's presence on pizza is a testament to the art of balancing boldness and harmony.

In the following chapters, we'll delve deeper into the world of pepperoni-infused pizzas, exploring classic recipes, inventive twists, and delightful combinations that showcase the versatile nature of this beloved ingredient.

Chapter 2: Mastering the Pizza Crust

The crust is the canvas upon which the artistry of a pizza comes to life. It's more than just a base; it's a fundamental element that determines the texture, flavor, and overall experience of each slice. In this chapter, we'll dive into the world of pizza crusts, exploring various types of crusts, techniques for crafting homemade dough, and tips to achieve the elusive balance between crispy and chewy perfection.

The Foundation of a Great Pizza: Types of Crusts

There's no one-size-fits-all approach when it comes to pizza crusts. The type of crust you choose can significantly influence the character of your pizza. From thin and crispy to deep-dish and hearty, the options are as diverse as your imagination.

Thin Crust: Light and delicate, this crust offers a delicate crunch that lets the toppings shine.

Thick Crust: Also known as pan or Sicilian style, this crust is hearty and doughy, providing a satisfying chew.

Stuffed Crust: An indulgent option where cheese is tucked into the edges, creating a gooey surprise with every bite.

Neapolitan Crust: Hailing from Naples, this classic crust is thin, soft, and slightly charred from the high heat of a wood-fired oven.

Gluten-Free Crust: Catering to dietary needs, this crust is made with alternative flours to provide a gluten-free option without compromising taste.

Crafting the Perfect Homemade Pizza Dough

Creating your own pizza dough is a rewarding experience that allows you to customize the flavor and texture of your crust. Here's a basic homemade pizza dough recipe to get you started:

Ingredients:

- 2 ¼ tsp active dry yeast
- 1 tsp sugar
- 1 ½ cups warm water
- 3 ½ cups all-purpose flour
- 2 tbsp olive oil
- 1 tsp salt

1. In a bowl, combine warm water, sugar, and yeast. Let it sit for about 5 minutes until it's frothy.
2. Add flour, olive oil, and salt. Mix until a dough forms.
3. Knead the dough on a floured surface for about 5-7 minutes until it's smooth and elastic.
4. Place the dough in a greased bowl, cover it, and let it rise for about 1-2 hours, or until it's doubled in size.
5. Punch down the dough, then turn it out onto a floured surface and shape it into your desired crust size.

Tips for Achieving Crispy and Chewy Crusts

Achieving the perfect crust texture requires careful attention to technique. Here are some tips to help you strike the ideal balance between crispiness and chewiness:

Preheat Your Oven: Ensure your oven is properly preheated to the highest temperature it can reach.

Use a Pizza Stone or Steel: Placing your pizza on a preheated stone or steel helps transfer heat directly to the crust, resulting in a crispy base.

Par-Bake the Crust: For toppings that require longer cooking times, consider partially baking the crust before adding toppings to avoid a soggy center.

Thinly Sliced Toppings: Thicker toppings release moisture during baking, potentially making the crust soggy. opt for thinly sliced ingredients and pre-cook high-moisture toppings like mushrooms.

Consider the Order of Toppings: Layering cheese over the sauce can act as a barrier, preventing moisture from seeping into the crust.

Don't Overload: While it's tempting to load up on toppings, a crowded pizza can lead to uneven cooking. Less is often more when it comes to pizza.

Mastering the art of pizza crust is a journey that combines technique with creativity. Whether you're drawn to the elegance of a thin crust or the hearty satisfaction of a deep-dish, understanding the nuances of crust types and perfecting your dough-making skills will elevate your pizza creations to new heights. As you experiment with crust thickness, toppings, and baking methods, you'll discover your personal pizza crust masterpiece.

In the upcoming chapters, we'll explore how to transform your expertly crafted crusts into delectable pepperoni-infused pizzas that will satisfy every craving.

Chapter 3: Classic Pepperoni Pizza

The classic pepperoni pizza stands as a testament to the timeless marriage of simple ingredients and bold flavors. In this chapter, we'll explore the art of crafting the quintessential pepperoni pizza, from a traditional Margherita base with a pepperoni twist to the delicate balance of cheese and pepperoni proportions. Additionally, we'll uncover baking techniques that result in a perfectly baked classic slice.

Traditional Margherita with Pepperoni Twist

The Margherita pizza, named after Queen Margherita of Italy, is a tribute to the colors of the Italian flag—red tomatoes, white mozzarella, and green basil. Adding a pepperoni twist to this classic offers a delightful fusion of flavors. Here's how to create this masterpiece:

Ingredients:

- Pizza dough (thin crust for authenticity)
- Tomato sauce or crushed San Marzano tomatoes
- Fresh mozzarella cheese, sliced
- Fresh basil leaves
- Pepperoni slices
- Olive oil
- Salt and pepper

Assembly:

1. Roll out the pizza dough to your desired thickness and size.
2. Spread a thin layer of tomato sauce over the dough.

3. Arrange slices of fresh mozzarella evenly.
4. Place fresh basil leaves between the cheese.
5. Add pepperoni slices, ensuring an even distribution.
6. Drizzle olive oil over the toppings and season with salt and pepper.

Baking:

1. Preheat your oven to its highest temperature.
2. If using a pizza stone or steel, place it in the oven during preheating.
3. Transfer the pizza onto a pizza peel or an inverted baking sheet dusted with flour or cornmeal.
4. Slide the pizza onto the preheated stone or steel in the oven.
5. Bake for about 8-10 minutes or until the crust is golden and the cheese is bubbly and slightly browned.

Balancing Cheese and Pepperoni Proportions

Achieving the perfect harmony between cheese and pepperoni is crucial for a balanced classic pepperoni pizza. Too much cheese can overpower the pepperoni's boldness, while too many pepperoni slices can make the pizza greasy. Aim for a ratio that allows both elements to shine.

Baking Techniques for the Classic Slice

The classic pepperoni pizza benefits from high heat and a relatively short baking time. Here are some baking techniques to ensure your classic slice is cooked to perfection:

Preheat and Preheat: Make sure your oven is thoroughly preheated. If using a pizza stone or steel, allow them to heat up as well.

Uniform Heat Distribution: Place the pizza in the center of the oven to ensure even cooking.

Watch the Cheese: Keep an eye on the cheese—when it's bubbly, slightly browned, and has that irresistible "stretch," the pizza is ready.

Rest and Slice: Allow the pizza to rest for a minute or two after baking. This prevents the cheese and toppings from sliding off when you slice it.

The classic pepperoni pizza takes the cherished elements of a Margherita and infuses them with the boldness of pepperoni. Its simplicity in design is a canvas for flavor exploration. By mastering the creation, balancing the cheese-pepperoni interplay, and perfecting the baking process, you'll uncover the essence of this iconic slice that has delighted generations.

In the next chapters, we'll venture beyond the classics, exploring gourmet pepperoni combinations and inventive twists that continue to evolve the pepperoni pizza experience.

Chapter 4: Pepperoni Calzone Creations

The calzone, a folded and stuffed cousin of the pizza, offers a unique way to enjoy the flavors of pepperoni-infused goodness. In this chapter, we'll embark on a journey of creating delightful pepperoni calzones. We'll explore various fillings, learn the art of crafting the perfect flaky and golden calzone dough, and discover dipping sauces that elevate the calzone experience.

Folded Delights: Calzones Filled with Pepperoni Goodness

Calzones are a perfect vessel for delivering a mouthful of flavors with every bite. Here's how to create a pepperoni-filled calzone that's sure to satisfy:

Ingredients:

- Pizza dough (homemade or store-bought)
- Tomato sauce for dipping
- Pepperoni slices
- Shredded mozzarella cheese
- Ricotta cheese
- Sliced black olives (optional)
- Sliced bell peppers (optional)
- Diced onions (optional)
- Olive oil
- Italian herbs (oregano, basil, thyme)
- Salt and pepper

Assembly:

1. Preheat your oven to the recommended temperature for the pizza dough.
2. Roll out a portion of pizza dough into a circle or rectangle, depending on your preference.
3. Spread a thin layer of tomato sauce over half of the dough.
4. Layer shredded mozzarella, ricotta, pepperoni, and any optional ingredients on the sauced half.
5. Sprinkle Italian herbs, salt, and pepper over the fillings.
6. Carefully fold the other half of the dough over the fillings, creating a half-moon shape.
7. Press and crimp the edges to seal the calzone.

Baking:

1. Place the calzone on a baking sheet or pizza stone.
2. Brush the top with olive oil for a golden finish.
3. Bake for the recommended time or until the calzone is golden brown and crispy.

Calzone Dough Perfection: Flaky and Golden

The calzone dough is key to achieving the desirable flaky and golden exterior. Here's a basic calzone dough recipe:

Ingredients:

- 2 ¼ tsp active dry yeast
- 1 tsp sugar
- 1 ½ cups warm water
- 4 cups all-purpose flour
- 2 tbsp olive oil
- 1 tsp salt

1. Mix warm water, sugar, and yeast. Let it sit for about 5 minutes until frothy.
2. Add flour, olive oil, and salt. Mix into a dough.
3. Knead for 5-7 minutes until smooth. Let it rise in a greased bowl until doubled.
4. Punch down the dough, divide, and shape into calzone-sized portions.

Dipping Sauces to Complement Your Calzone

Dipping sauces enhance the calzone experience. Consider these options:

Marinara Sauce: A classic choice that complements the flavors of the fillings.

Garlic Butter: Infused with herbs, it adds richness and aroma.

Pesto: Adds a fresh, herbaceous dimension.

Spicy Ranch: Offers a creamy and tangy kick.

Pepperoni calzones combine the convenience of a handheld meal with the indulgence of a pizza. Their flaky exterior encases a world of flavors, creating a savory pocket of joy. By exploring diverse fillings, perfecting the calzone dough, and pairing with delectable dipping sauces, you'll create an experience that's both comforting and exciting.

In the next chapters, we'll delve deeper into gourmet pepperoni combinations and explore the art of crafting pepperoni-infused pizzas that push the boundaries of flavor.

Chapter 5: Exploring Gourmet Pepperoni Combinations

Elevating the humble pepperoni pizza to a gourmet experience involves an artful exploration of flavors and ingredients. In this chapter, we embark on a journey of gourmet pepperoni combinations. We'll delve into the world of premium cheeses and herbs that harmonize with pepperoni, experiment with creative toppings that elevate the pizza experience, and uncover unique flavor profiles that are sure to impress both your taste buds and your guests.

Pairing Pepperoni with Premium Cheeses and Herbs

The interplay between pepperoni, premium cheeses, and aromatic herbs can create a symphony of tastes. Here are some combinations to consider:

Gouda and Thyme: Smoky Gouda and the earthy notes of thyme complement the boldness of pepperoni.

Blue Cheese and Rosemary: The sharp tang of blue cheese balances the richness of pepperoni, while rosemary adds depth.

Fontina and Basil: The nuttiness of Fontina pairs well with the sweetness of basil, enhancing the flavors of pepperoni.

Creative Toppings for an Elevated Experience

Elevating a pepperoni pizza involves thinking outside the box. Here are some creative toppings to consider:

Arugula Salad: Top your pizza with fresh arugula tossed in lemon vinaigrette after baking for a burst of freshness.

Truffle Oil: Drizzle truffle oil over your pizza for a luxurious and aromatic touch.

Caramelized Onions: The sweetness of caramelized onions complements the spiciness of pepperoni.

Figs or Dates: Add slices of fresh figs or dates for a delightful sweet contrast.

Impressing Guests with Unique Flavor Profiles

When hosting a gathering, unique flavor profiles can make a lasting impression. Consider these combinations:

Pear and Prosciutto: Combining thinly sliced pears, salty prosciutto, and pepperoni creates a sweet-savory medley.

Honey and Chili Flakes: A drizzle of honey and a sprinkle of chili flakes offer a balanced blend of sweetness and heat.

Balsamic Reduction: A drizzle of balsamic reduction can add complexity and depth to the flavors.

Gourmet pepperoni combinations unlock a world of culinary creativity, allowing you to explore an array of flavors that harmonize with the boldness of pepperoni. Whether you're pairing with premium cheeses and aromatic herbs, experimenting with unique toppings, or crafting pizzas with distinct flavor profiles, the journey to gourmet pepperoni pizzas is one of discovery and delight.

Chapter 6: Homemade vs. Store-Bought Pepperoni

The pepperoni you choose can significantly impact the flavor and quality of your pizza. In this chapter, we'll explore the two sides of the pepperoni spectrum—crafting your own artisanal pepperoni at home and navigating the aisles to select high-quality store-bought options. Additionally, we'll conduct a taste test to compare the merits of homemade and store-bought pepperoni in a showdown that showcases the artistry and convenience of both choices.

Crafting Your Own Artisanal Pepperoni at Home

Crafting your own pepperoni allows you to tailor the flavors and ingredients to your liking. Here's a basic recipe for homemade pepperoni:

Ingredients:

- 1 lb ground pork
- 1 tsp salt
- 1 tsp paprika
- 1 tsp garlic powder
- 1 tsp crushed red pepper flakes
- 1/2 tsp black pepper
- 1/2 tsp fennel seeds
- 1/4 tsp cayenne pepper (adjust to taste)

1. Combine all the ingredients in a bowl and mix thoroughly.
2. If using a sausage stuffer, stuff the mixture into casings. If not, shape the mixture into a log using plastic wrap.

3. If using casings, tie off the ends and let the sausage rest in the refrigerator overnight.

4. If using the log method, wrap the log tightly in plastic wrap and let it rest in the refrigerator overnight.

5. Once cured, your homemade pepperoni is ready to be sliced and used on your pizzas.

Navigating the Aisles: Selecting Quality Store-Bought Pepperoni

Selecting store-bought pepperoni involves considering factors such as ingredients, texture, and flavor. Look for options that use natural casing and quality meats, and avoid products with excessive additives or fillers. Opt for brands that prioritize traditional curing methods, resulting in a product that closely resembles the artisanal process.

Taste Test: Homemade vs. Store-Bought Showdown

Conducting a taste test allows you to appreciate the nuances of homemade and store-bought pepperoni. Prepare two identical pizzas—one with your homemade pepperoni and the other with your chosen store-bought option. Consider aspects such as flavor, texture, spiciness, and overall satisfaction. The taste test is a fun way to explore the distinct characteristics of each type of pepperoni.

The decision between homemade and store-bought pepperoni involves a balance between creativity and convenience. Crafting your own artisanal pepperoni empowers you to experiment with flavors and ingredients, creating a personalized touch. On the other hand, selecting quality store-bought options provides a convenient solution that doesn't compromise on taste.

In the upcoming chapters, we'll explore gluten-free pepperoni pizza variations, healthier twists, and innovative fusion creations that continue to showcase the versatility of pepperoni.

Chapter 7: Gluten-Free Pepperoni Pizza Options

For those who follow a gluten-free diet, the joy of indulging in a delicious pepperoni pizza shouldn't be off the table. In this chapter, we'll delve into the realm of gluten-free pepperoni pizza options. We'll explore alternative crusts, share recipes for gluten-free dough, discuss strategies to ensure cross-contamination-free preparation, and guide you toward enjoying flavorful gluten-free pizzas that cater to your dietary needs.

Gluten-Free Crust Alternatives and Recipes

Embracing a gluten-free lifestyle doesn't mean giving up on your love for pizza. There are several alternative crust options that deliver both taste and texture:

Cauliflower Crust: Made from finely grated cauliflower, this crust offers a unique flavor and a slightly crisp texture.

Almond Flour Crust: Almond flour lends a nutty richness to the crust while creating a golden-brown exterior.

Quinoa Crust: A protein-rich choice that provides a hearty base for your pizza toppings.

Pre-Made Gluten-Free Crusts: Many grocery stores now offer pre-made gluten-free crusts, providing a convenient solution.

Ensuring Cross-Contamination-Free Preparation

When preparing gluten-free pizzas, preventing cross-contamination is crucial. Follow these steps to ensure a safe cooking environment:

Clean Work Surface: Thoroughly clean and sanitize your work surface before beginning.

Separate Utensils: Use separate utensils and cutting boards that have not been in contact with gluten-containing ingredients.

Gluten-Free Ingredients: Carefully read labels to ensure all ingredients, including sauces and seasonings, are certified gluten-free.

Dedicated Oven Space: If possible, use a separate oven or oven-safe pan to prevent cross-contamination.

Enjoying Flavorful Gluten-Free Pizzas

Creating flavorful gluten-free pizzas involves layering complementary ingredients that balance textures and tastes:

Sauce Variety: Experiment with different sauces, from classic tomato to pesto or garlic-infused olive oil.

Premium Cheeses: opt for high-quality cheeses like fresh mozzarella, goat cheese, or aged cheddar to enhance the flavors.

Herbs and Spices: Add depth and aroma with a variety of herbs and spices such as basil, oregano, thyme, and red pepper flakes.

Assorted Toppings: Explore a range of toppings, from sautéed mushrooms to caramelized onions and roasted red peppers.

Gluten-free pepperoni pizzas open up a world of possibilities for those with dietary restrictions. By exploring alternative crusts, ensuring cross-contamination-free preparation, and embracing a diverse range of flavors, you can enjoy delicious and satisfying gluten-free pizzas that cater to your taste buds and nutritional needs.

In the upcoming chapters, we'll continue to explore healthier variations, inventive fusion twists, and international interpretations that showcase the versatility of pepperoni on pizza.

Chapter 8: Healthier Twist: Lean Turkey Pepperoni Pizzas

Healthy eating doesn't mean sacrificing the joy of pizza. In this chapter, we'll explore a healthier twist on traditional pepperoni pizzas—lean turkey pepperoni pizzas. We'll delve into the benefits of reducing fat with turkey pepperoni swaps, discuss lighter cheese choices and the abundance of veggies that enhance nutrition, and guide you toward guilt-free pizza indulgence that keeps your taste buds and health in mind.

Reducing Fat with Turkey Pepperoni Swaps

Swapping classic pepperoni with lean turkey pepperoni is a simple yet effective way to reduce fat and calories while retaining the beloved flavors. Turkey pepperoni offers a leaner protein source that's lower in saturated fat, making it an ideal choice for those looking to make healthier choices without sacrificing taste.

Lighter Cheese Choices and Veggie Abundance

Opting for lighter cheese choices helps cut down on saturated fat while maintaining the cheesy goodness. Consider these options:

Part-Skim Mozzarella: A versatile cheese that melts beautifully and adds a creamy texture without excess fat.

Feta: Crumbly and flavorful, feta brings a tangy punch to your pizza without being overly indulgent.

Goat Cheese: Creamy and slightly tangy, goat cheese adds a gourmet touch to your pizza.

Embrace the vibrancy of vegetables to elevate both the nutritional profile and taste of your pizza. Load up on veggies like bell peppers, spinach, tomatoes, onions, and mushrooms to add a variety of flavors, textures, and nutrients.

Guilt-Free Pizza Indulgence

Creating guilt-free pizzas involves balance and mindfulness:

Portion Control: Enjoy your pizza in moderation, savoring each bite without overindulging.

Thin Crusts: Opt for thin or whole grain crusts to reduce calorie intake while still enjoying the pizza experience.

Lean Proteins: In addition to turkey pepperoni, consider adding grilled chicken or lean turkey sausage for added protein.

Lean turkey pepperoni pizzas offer a healthier twist on the classic favorite, allowing you to enjoy the comfort of pizza without compromising your health goals. By swapping out higher-fat ingredients, choosing lighter cheeses, and embracing the abundance of vegetables, you can create pizzas that not only satisfy your taste buds but also nourish your body.

Chapter 9: Spicy Sensations: Jalapeño and Pepperoni Pizzas

For those who crave a fiery kick on their pizza, the combination of jalapeños and pepperoni delivers a tantalizing explosion of heat and flavor. In this chapter, we'll explore the art of creating spicy sensations with jalapeño and pepperoni pizzas. We'll delve into the delicate balance between heat and flavor, consider creative options for incorporating other spicy pepper varieties, and introduce refreshing pairings that tame the spice for a well-rounded culinary experience.

Balancing Heat and Flavor with Jalapeños

Jalapeños bring both heat and a unique vegetal flavor to your pizza. To achieve the perfect balance between spice and taste:

Slicing and Seeding: When working with jalapeños, consider slicing and deseeding them to control their heat level. The seeds and membranes are the spiciest parts, so removing them can moderate the overall heat.

Even Distribution: For an even distribution of heat, scatter the jalapeño slices strategically across the pizza. This ensures that every bite has a harmonious blend of flavors.

Flavor Harmony: Pair jalapeños with ingredients that complement their heat. Sweet peppers, like bell peppers or mini sweet peppers, can add a touch of sweetness to offset the spice.

Creative Heat: Other Spicy Pepper Options

For those looking to explore a wider spectrum of spiciness, consider incorporating other pepper varieties that offer unique heat levels and flavors:

Serrano Peppers: Serranos are slightly hotter than jalapeños and carry a crisp, bright flavor. Their moderate heat can provide an exciting upgrade to your pizza.

Habanero Peppers: If you're seeking a thrilling experience, habaneros bring intense heat with fruity undertones. Use them sparingly for a fiery adventure.

Ghost Peppers (Bhut Jolokia): For the most daring, ghost peppers bring extreme heat with smoky and earthy notes. Use ghost peppers cautiously and only if you're accustomed to handling extreme spice.

Refreshing Pairings to Tame the Spice

While the heat of jalapeños and other spicy peppers is exhilarating, pairing them with refreshing elements can provide balance and contrast:

Cooling Dairy: Incorporate creamy elements like dollops of ricotta cheese or spoonfuls of yogurt onto the pizza. The creamy texture helps temper the heat and provides a cooling effect.

Citrus Zest: The bright zest of lemon or lime can counterbalance the heat with its zesty tang. Sprinkle citrus zest over the finished pizza to create an invigorating contrast.

Fresh Herbs: Mint, cilantro, and parsley bring a refreshing burst of flavor that complements the heat. Their herbal notes add layers of complexity to the pizza's profile.

Jalapeño and pepperoni pizzas offer a journey into the world of heat and flavor, where the bite of spice meets the richness of pepperoni. By mastering the balance between heat and taste, exploring a variety of spicy pepper options, and experimenting with refreshing pairings, you can create pizzas that ignite the senses and satisfy the palate.

In the upcoming chapters, we'll continue to explore international influences, inventive fusion twists, and unique flavor combinations that showcase the versatility of pepperoni on pizza.

Chapter 10: Breakfast Delight: Pepperoni and Egg Pizza

Who says pizza is just for lunch and dinner? In this chapter, we'll explore the delightful world of breakfast-themed pizzas featuring the dynamic duo of pepperoni and eggs. We'll dive into creating sunrise slices that infuse morning flavors onto your pizza, discuss techniques to achieve the perfectly runny egg topping, and introduce morning beverage pairings that enhance your pizza brunch experience.

Sunrise Slices: Breakfast-Themed Pizzas

Bringing breakfast to your pizza involves combining traditional morning ingredients with the beloved flavors of pepperoni. Consider these breakfast-themed toppings:

Sausage: Crumbled breakfast sausage adds a hearty and savory element to your morning pizza.

Bacon: Crispy bacon bits provide a smoky and salty contrast to the richness of eggs and cheese.

Potatoes: Sliced or diced potatoes bring a satisfying starchiness to your pizza, reminiscent of breakfast hash.

Green Vegetables: Spinach, kale, or broccoli florets add a burst of color and nutrients to your pizza.

Achieving the Perfectly Runny Egg on Pizza

Mastering the art of a perfectly runny egg on pizza requires precision and timing:

Precook the Crust: Prebake the pizza crust slightly before adding the toppings. This prevents the egg from becoming overcooked while the crust bakes.

Create Indentation: Use the back of a spoon to create a well or indentation in the center of the pizza for the egg.

Crack the Egg: Crack a fresh egg into the well you've created, taking care not to break the yolk.

Season: Sprinkle salt, pepper, and any desired herbs over the egg to enhance its flavor.

Bake Briefly: Return the pizza to the oven and bake until the egg whites are set but the yolk remains runny. The goal is a creamy, luscious yolk that adds richness to the pizza.

Morning Beverage Pairings for Your Pizza Brunch

Enhance your breakfast pizza experience with well-paired morning beverages:

Freshly Brewed Coffee: The classic morning pick-me-up that pairs well with the savory and indulgent nature of breakfast pizza.

Fruit Juices: Freshly squeezed orange juice or a refreshing grapefruit juice adds a burst of citrus to complement the pizza's flavors.

Herbal Teas: Light and fragrant herbal teas like chamomile or mint provide a soothing contrast to the savory pizza.

Pepperoni and egg breakfast pizzas offer a delightful departure from the ordinary morning meal, infusing your day with the flavors of a cozy breakfast. By crafting sunrise slices, mastering the technique of achieving the perfectly runny egg topping, and exploring beverage pairings that complement your pizza brunch, you'll create a morning dining experience that's both comforting and exciting.

In the upcoming chapters, we'll continue to explore international influences, inventive fusion twists, and unique flavor combinations that showcase the versatility of pepperoni on pizza.

Chapter 11: Veggie Harmony: Roasted Veggie and Pepperoni Pizzas

Vegetables and pepperoni may seem like an unconventional pair, but the harmony they create on a pizza is a symphony of flavors. In this chapter, we'll explore the art of crafting roasted veggie and pepperoni pizzas. We'll delve into roasting techniques that enhance the flavors of vegetables, discuss pepperoni's complementary role in veggie-centric pies, and explore herb and spice infusions that elevate your pizza to a new level of deliciousness.

Roasting Techniques for Flavor-Packed Veggies

Roasting vegetables brings out their natural sweetness and intensifies their flavors. To master the art of roasting for pizza:

Uniform Slicing: Slice your vegetables into uniform pieces to ensure even cooking.

Toss with Oil: Toss the veggies with olive oil, salt, and pepper before roasting to enhance their flavor.

High Heat: Roast at a high temperature (around 425°F/ 220°C) for a balance of caramelization and tenderness.

Single Layer: Spread the vegetables in a single layer on the baking sheet to avoid steaming and promote browning.

Pepperoni's Complementary Role with Veggies

Pepperoni plays a complementary role when paired with roasted vegetables, offering a savory and slightly spicy contrast to the sweetness of the veggies. The umami-rich notes of pepperoni can enhance the overall depth of flavor in veggie-centric pizzas.

Herb and Spice Infusions for Veggie-Centric Pizzas

Elevate your roasted veggie and pepperoni pizzas with herb and spice infusions that enhance the vegetable medley:

Fresh Basil: Fragrant basil adds a burst of freshness that complements the roasted flavors.

Thyme and Rosemary: Earthy and aromatic, thyme and rosemary enhance the savory notes of the pizza.

Red Pepper Flakes: A touch of heat from red pepper flakes balances the sweetness of roasted vegetables.

Garlic Infusion: Drizzle garlic-infused olive oil over the pizza for a mellow garlic flavor.

Roasted veggie and pepperoni pizzas bring together the best of both worlds—sweetness from roasted vegetables and savory richness from pepperoni. By mastering roasting techniques for flavor-packed veggies, appreciating pepperoni's complementary role, and infusing your pizza with the right herbs and spices, you'll create pizzas that are a celebration of harmonious flavors.

In the upcoming chapters, we'll continue to explore international influences, inventive fusion twists, and unique flavor combinations that showcase the versatility of pepperoni on pizza.

Chapter 12: Pepperoni Pizza Party Bites for Kids

Pizza parties are a hit with kids, and pepperoni pizza bites bring a fun and delicious twist to the celebration. In this chapter, we'll explore the world of mini pepperoni pizzas designed to delight the little ones. We'll dive into creating kid-friendly shapes and themes that capture their imagination, and provide tips for hosting a pepperoni pizza party that's both entertaining and flavorful.

Mini Pepperoni Pizzas for Little Ones

Mini pepperoni pizzas are a fantastic way to cater to kids' appetites and preferences. Consider these options:

English Muffin Pizzas: Using halved English muffins as the base, kids can assemble their own mini pizzas.

Tortilla Pizzas: Small tortillas can serve as a quick and easy pizza crust, perfect for little hands.

Bagel Pizzas: Bagel halves transform into mini pizza crusts, ready to be topped with favorite ingredients.

Pita Pocket Pizzas: Pita pockets provide a fun and portable option for mini pizza creations.

Kid-Friendly Shapes and Themes

Captivate kids' attention with playful shapes and themes that make mealtime exciting:

Animal Faces: Use pepperoni slices for eyes, olives for noses, and bell pepper strips for smiles to create adorable animal faces on the mini pizzas.

Star Power: Use star-shaped cookie cutters to create star-themed pepperoni pizza bites that shine.

Emoji Embrace: Turn mini pizzas into expressive emojis using various toppings to create familiar faces.

Rainbow Pizza: Arrange colorful veggies in a rainbow pattern on the mini pizzas to create a visually appealing and nutritious treat.

Hosting a Pepperoni Pizza Party for Kids

Hosting a pepperoni pizza party for kids is a guaranteed hit:

Pizza Station: Set up a pizza-making station with prepped ingredients so kids can build their own mini pizzas.

Crafty Decorations: Embrace the pizza theme with pizza-inspired decorations and table settings.

Pepperoni Pizza Crafts: Engage kids with pizza-themed crafts, like creating their own paper plate pizzas or designing pizza box art.

Sweet Endings: Offer mini dessert pizzas using sugar cookie dough as the base and topped with fruit and sweet sauces.

Pepperoni pizza party bites for kids infuse excitement into mealtime and celebrations. By creating mini pepperoni pizzas tailored to their preferences, exploring kid-friendly shapes and themes, and hosting a lively pepperoni pizza party, you'll provide an unforgettable experience that combines fun, flavor, and creativity.

In the upcoming chapters, we'll continue to explore international influences, inventive fusion twists, and unique flavor combinations that showcase the versatility of pepperoni on pizza.

Chapter 13: International Flair: Pepperoni Variations Around the World

Pepperoni pizza knows no borders—it's a beloved classic that has inspired creative interpretations around the world. In this chapter, we'll embark on a culinary journey to explore pepperoni variations from different corners of the globe. We'll delve into unusual toppings inspired by various culinary traditions, and provide guidance on adapting authentic recipes to your home kitchen, allowing you to savor the international flair of pepperoni pizza.

Exploring Global Pepperoni Pizza Interpretations

Pepperoni pizza has found its way into the hearts of people worldwide, each culture adding its own unique twist:

Italian-Inspired Pepperoni: Journey to the birthplace of pizza with an Italian-inspired creation. Layer the pizza with slices of pepperoni, crumbled Italian sausage, roasted red peppers, and fresh mozzarella. Top with a handful of fresh basil leaves before serving.

Mexican Fusion: Immerse yourself in bold Mexican flavors. Top your pizza with spicy chorizo, black beans, roasted corn, and sliced avocado. A drizzle of tangy lime crema adds a zesty finish.

Mediterranean Infusion: Embark on a culinary tour of the Mediterranean. Spread hummus over the pizza crust, then layer with pepperoni, crumbled feta cheese, Kalamata olives, red onion slices, and cherry tomatoes. Finish with a drizzle of tzatziki sauce.

Italian-Inspired Pepperoni Pizza

Ingredients:

- Pizza dough (pre-made or homemade)
- Tomato sauce
- Sliced pepperoni
- Crumbled Italian sausage
- Roasted red pepper strips
- Fresh mozzarella, sliced
- Fresh basil leaves
- Olive oil
- Salt and pepper

Instructions:

1. Preheat your oven according to the pizza dough instructions.
2. Roll out the pizza dough onto a baking sheet or pizza stone.
3. Spread a thin layer of tomato sauce over the dough.
4. Arrange slices of pepperoni, crumbled Italian sausage, and roasted red pepper strips evenly over the sauce.
5. Top with slices of fresh mozzarella.
6. Drizzle a bit of olive oil over the toppings and season with salt and pepper.
7. Bake the pizza in the preheated oven until the crust is golden and the cheese is bubbly.
8. Remove from the oven and sprinkle fresh basil leaves over the pizza.
9. Let the pizza cool slightly before slicing and serving.

Mexican Fusion Pepperoni Pizza
   Ingredients:

- Pizza dough (pre-made or homemade)
- Spicy tomato sauce or salsa
- Sliced pepperoni
- Cooked spicy chorizo
- Black beans, drained and rinsed
- Roasted corn kernels
- Sliced avocado
- Lime crema (mix sour cream with lime juice and zest)
- Fresh cilantro leaves
- Salt and pepper

Instructions:

1. Preheat your oven according to the pizza dough instructions.
2. Roll out the pizza dough onto a baking sheet or pizza stone.
3. Spread a layer of spicy tomato sauce or salsa over the dough.
4. Arrange slices of pepperoni, cooked spicy chorizo, black beans, and roasted corn evenly over the sauce.
5. Bake the pizza in the preheated oven until the crust is golden.
6. Remove from the oven and top with sliced avocado.
7. Drizzle lime crema over the toppings and season with salt and pepper.
8. Garnish with fresh cilantro leaves.
9. Allow the pizza to cool slightly before cutting and

serving.

Mediterranean-Inspired Pepperoni Pizza

Ingredients:

- Pizza dough (pre-made or homemade)
- Hummus
- Sliced pepperoni
- Crumbled feta cheese
- Kalamata olives, pitted and sliced
- Red onion slices
- Cherry tomatoes, halved
- Tzatziki sauce
- Fresh oregano leaves
- Olive oil
- Salt and pepper

Instructions:

1. Preheat your oven according to the pizza dough instructions.
2. Roll out the pizza dough onto a baking sheet or pizza stone.
3. Spread a layer of hummus over the dough.
4. Arrange slices of pepperoni, crumbled feta cheese, Kalamata olives, red onion slices, and cherry tomato halves over the hummus.
5. Bake the pizza in the preheated oven until the crust is crispy and the cheese is melted.

6. Remove from the oven and drizzle tzatziki sauce over the toppings.
7. Sprinkle fresh oregano leaves over the pizza.
8. Finish with a drizzle of olive oil and season with salt and pepper.
9. Let the pizza cool slightly before slicing and serving.

Unusual Toppings from Different Culinary Traditions

Dive into unusual toppings that showcase the culinary diversity of pepperoni pizza:

Indian Fusion: Embrace the vibrancy of Indian cuisine. Top your pizza with tandoori-spiced pepperoni, cubes of paneer cheese, colorful bell pepper strips, and a sprinkling of fresh cilantro. Serve with a side of mint chutney for dipping.

Scandinavian Surprises: Discover the elegance of Scandinavian flavors. Layer smoked salmon over the pizza, then sprinkle with fresh dill and capers. After baking, add dollops of crème fraiche for a luxurious touch.

Middle Eastern Medley: Indulge in the rich flavors of the Middle East. Top your pizza with seasoned ground lamb, a tomato sauce infused with harissa, pomegranate arils, and crumbled feta cheese. A sprinkle of sumac adds a final burst of flavor.

Adapting Authentic Recipes to Home Kitchens

Bringing international flavors to your home kitchen involves understanding and adapting authentic recipes:

Ingredient Substitutions: When certain ingredients are hard to find, don't hesitate to make substitutions that align with the spirit of the dish. For example, if paneer is unavailable, substitute with a mild white cheese like mozzarella.

Homemade Sauces: Elevate your pizzas with homemade sauces that capture the essence of each cuisine. Prepare marinara with fresh tomatoes, garlic, and basil for an Italian touch, or mix yogurt with lemon juice and herbs for a Mediterranean-inspired drizzle.

Cultural Accents: Enhance the experience with cultural accents. Serve Italian-inspired pizza with a side of extra virgin olive oil and balsamic vinegar for dipping, or pair Middle Eastern pizza with warm pita bread.

Exploring pepperoni variations from around the world brings a sense of adventure and cultural appreciation to your pizza experience. By embracing global inspirations, experimenting with unusual toppings, and adapting authentic recipes to your home kitchen, you'll embark on a culinary journey that showcases the universal appeal of pepperoni pizza.

In the upcoming chapters, we'll continue to explore inventive fusion twists, unique flavor combinations, and practical tips to master the art of creating perfect pepperoni pizzas.

Chapter 14: Fusion Fiesta: Pepperoni Pizza-Inspired Dishes

The irresistible flavors of pepperoni pizza can transcend the boundaries of a traditional slice and inspire a fusion of culinary creations. In this chapter, we'll celebrate the fusion fiesta by exploring how to incorporate beloved pizza flavors into various dishes. We'll delve into crafting pepperoni pizza burgers, pastas, and more, unleashing your fusion food creativity and inviting you on exciting culinary adventures.

Incorporating Pizza Flavors into Other Dishes

The essence of pepperoni pizza can infuse its flavors into unexpected dishes:

Pepperoni Pizza Flatbreads: Transform the flavors of a pizza into a flatbread. Spread tomato sauce on a flatbread, top with shredded mozzarella, pepperoni slices, and diced bell peppers. Bake until the cheese melts and the edges are crisp.

Pizza-Inspired Omelets: Enhance your breakfast routine by folding pepperoni, shredded cheese, and sautéed bell peppers into an omelet. The result is a savory and satisfying morning delight.

Pepperoni Pizza Quesadillas: Elevate your quesadillas by filling them with pepperoni, mozzarella, and marinara sauce. The fusion of Italian and Mexican flavors will be a hit.

Pepperoni Pizza Flatbreads
Ingredients:

- Flatbread or naan
- Tomato sauce

- Shredded mozzarella cheese
- Pepperoni slices
- Diced bell peppers
- Fresh basil leaves
- Olive oil
- Salt and pepper

Instructions:

1. Preheat your oven according to the flatbread instructions.
2. Place the flatbread on a baking sheet or pizza stone.
3. Spread a thin layer of tomato sauce over the flatbread.
4. Sprinkle a generous amount of shredded mozzarella cheese over the sauce.
5. Arrange pepperoni slices and diced bell peppers evenly over the cheese.
6. Drizzle a bit of olive oil over the toppings and season with salt and pepper.
7. Bake the flatbread in the preheated oven until the cheese is melted and bubbly.
8. Remove from the oven and sprinkle fresh basil leaves over the flatbread.
9. Let it cool for a minute before slicing and serving.

Pizza-Inspired Omelet

Ingredients:

- Eggs (2-3 per omelet)
- Salt and pepper
- Butter or oil for cooking
- Sliced pepperoni
- Shredded mozzarella cheese
- Diced bell peppers
- Chopped fresh basil

Instructions:

1. In a bowl, beat the eggs and season with salt and pepper.
2. Heat a non-stick skillet over medium heat and add butter or oil.
3. Pour the beaten eggs into the skillet and swirl to evenly coat the pan.
4. As the eggs begin to set, arrange sliced pepperoni, shredded mozzarella cheese, and diced bell peppers on one half of the omelet.
5. Fold the other half of the omelet over the toppings and press gently with a spatula.
6. Cook for another minute until the cheese is melted and the omelet is cooked through.
7. Slide the omelet onto a plate and garnish with chopped fresh basil.
8. Serve the pizza-inspired omelet hot

Pepperoni Pizza Quesadillas

Ingredients:

- Flour tortillas
- Marinara sauce
- Shredded mozzarella cheese
- Sliced pepperoni
- Olive oil
- Optional: crushed red pepper flakes

Instructions:

1. Lay a tortilla flat on a clean surface.
2. Spread a thin layer of marinara sauce over half of the tortilla.
3. Sprinkle a generous amount of shredded mozzarella cheese over the sauce.
4. Arrange sliced pepperoni over the cheese.
5. Fold the other half of the tortilla over the toppings to create a half-moon shape.
6. Heat a non-stick skillet over medium heat and add a drizzle of olive oil.
7. Carefully place the quesadilla in the skillet and cook for a few minutes on each side until the tortilla is golden and the cheese is melted.
8. Remove from the skillet, slice into wedges, and serve hot.
9. If desired, sprinkle crushed red pepper flakes over the quesadilla for an extra kick.

Pepperoni Pizza Burgers, Pastas, and More

The fusion fiesta extends to burgers, pastas, and beyond:

Pepperoni Pizza Burgers: Combine the elements of a pepperoni pizza with a juicy burger. Top your burger patty with pepperoni slices, marinara sauce, melted mozzarella, and fresh basil leaves.

Pizza Pasta Bake: Create a comforting casserole by mixing cooked pasta with marinara sauce, diced pepperoni, and shredded mozzarella. Bake until bubbly and golden for a pasta dish reminiscent of pizza.

Pepperoni Pizza-Stuffed Peppers: Fill bell pepper halves with a mixture of cooked ground beef, rice, marinara sauce, and diced pepperoni. Top with mozzarella cheese and bake until the peppers are tender and the cheese melts.

Fusion Food Creativity and Culinary Adventures

Fusion food is a playground for your culinary creativity:

Flavor Pairings: Experiment with unexpected flavor pairings. Incorporate the smokiness of bacon or the creaminess of ricotta cheese to enhance the pizza-inspired dishes.

Texture Contrast: Play with textures. Add crispy fried pepperoni as a topping to add crunch to salads or pasta dishes.

Cultural Connections: Draw inspiration from different cuisines. Fuse the flavors of pepperoni pizza with the spices of Indian cuisine or the herbs of French cooking for a unique experience.

The fusion fiesta takes the essence of pepperoni pizza to new culinary heights, where creativity knows no limits. By incorporating pizza flavors into unexpected dishes, crafting pepperoni pizza burgers, pastas, and more, and exploring fusion food creativity, you'll embark on a journey of flavor innovation that transforms the familiar into the extraordinary.

In the upcoming chapters, we'll continue to explore inventive twists, unique flavor combinations, and practical tips to master the art of creating perfect pepperoni pizzas.

Chapter 15: Artisanal Delights: Fresh Mozzarella and Pepperoni Pizzas

Elevate your pizza experience to new heights by embracing the creamy elegance of fresh mozzarella paired with the bold flavors of pepperoni. In this chapter, we'll explore the art of crafting artisanal pizzas that celebrate the harmony between these high-quality ingredients. We'll delve into the nuances of using fresh mozzarella, discuss how it elevates flavors, and provide tips for achieving the perfect melt that turns your pizza into a masterpiece.

The Creamy Elegance of Fresh Mozzarella

Fresh mozzarella is a delicate and luxurious cheese that transforms pizzas:

Texture: Fresh mozzarella's soft and creamy texture creates a delightful contrast to the crispy crust, offering a mouthwatering combination of sensations with every bite.

Mild Flavor: The mild and slightly sweet flavor of fresh mozzarella serves as a perfect canvas for the bold flavors of pepperoni to shine, making it an ideal companion on your pizza journey.

Melting Qualities: One of the joys of using fresh mozzarella is its exceptional melting qualities. When heated, it forms a rich, velvety layer that coats the pizza in a luscious embrace.

Elevating Flavors with High-Quality Ingredients

The marriage of fresh mozzarella and pepperoni leads to a symphony of flavors:

Saltiness and Creaminess: The natural saltiness of pepperoni marries beautifully with the creamy, subtle saltiness of fresh mozzarella, creating a balanced and indulgent flavor profile.

Pepperoni's Richness: The rich and slightly spicy notes of pepperoni enhance the mildness of fresh mozzarella, resulting in a layered taste experience that is both comforting and exciting.

Herb and Spice Pairings: Elevate your artisanal pizza by pairing fresh mozzarella and pepperoni with complementary herbs like fragrant basil or earthy oregano. Add a dash of red pepper flakes for a touch of heat that dances alongside the cheese and pepperoni.

Tips for Achieving the Perfect Mozzarella Melt

Master the art of achieving a flawless melt when working with fresh mozzarella:

Thin Slices: When using fresh mozzarella, slice it thinly to ensure that it melts evenly across the pizza, allowing every inch to be kissed by its creamy goodness.

Blotting: If your fresh mozzarella is particularly moist, gently blot it with paper towels before placing it on the pizza. This prevents excess moisture that could lead to a soggy crust.

Strategically Layering: As you assemble your pizza, place fresh mozzarella slices with care, ensuring they're spread evenly to avoid clumping. Leave a bit of space between slices to allow for even melting.

Balancing Ingredients: Achieve harmony by carefully balancing the amount of fresh mozzarella and pepperoni on the pizza. Their partnership should be a dance of flavors, enhancing each other without overwhelming the palate.

Creating artisanal pizzas that showcase the luxurious creaminess of fresh mozzarella alongside the bold flavors of pepperoni is a journey into culinary excellence. By understanding the nuances of fresh mozzarella, appreciating how it elevates flavors, and mastering the techniques for achieving the perfect melt, you'll embark on a path of pizza perfection that embraces the artistry of high-quality ingredients.

In the upcoming chapters, we'll continue to explore inventive twists, unique flavor combinations, and practical tips to master the art of creating perfect pepperoni pizzas.

Chapter 16: Pizzadillas: Where Pizza Meets Quesadilla

Prepare to embark on a flavor adventure as we merge the worlds of pizza and quesadillas to create the ultimate culinary fusion: the pizzadilla. In this chapter, we'll explore the creative realm where cheesy pizzas and crispy quesadillas collide. Discover the best of both worlds by perfecting the art of crafting pizzadillas, folding them to crispy perfection, and pairing them with delicious dips and salsas for a taste explosion.

The Best of Both Worlds: Pizza and Quesadilla Fusion

The pizzadilla is a delightful union of two beloved dishes:

Pizza's Flavors: Incorporate the familiar flavors of pizza, including pepperoni, gooey cheese, and marinara sauce, while embracing the art of layering ingredients for optimal flavor distribution.

Quesadilla's Crunch: Enjoy the satisfying crunch of a quesadilla, with tortillas that encase the cheesy goodness and turn golden and crispy during cooking.

Foldable and Crunchy: Perfecting the Pizzadilla Technique

Master the art of crafting the perfect pizzadilla:

Layering Technique: Begin by placing a tortilla on a heated skillet over medium heat. Spread a thin layer of marinara sauce, then sprinkle a generous amount of shredded mozzarella cheese over the sauce.

Pepperoni and Beyond: Arrange pepperoni slices over the cheese, adding a layer of robust flavor. Get creative by incorporating additional toppings such as sautéed mushrooms, diced onions, or sliced black olives.

Second Tortilla: Place a second tortilla over the toppings, creating a "sandwich" with the fillings in between. Press down gently with a spatula to help the tortillas adhere.

Crisp Perfection: Cook the pizzadilla for a few minutes on each side until the tortillas turn golden brown and crispy, and the cheese melts into a gooey delight. To facilitate even cooking, you can cover the skillet with a lid for a short period to ensure the cheese fully melts.

Dips and Salsas for Pizzadilla Pairing

Enhance your pizzadilla experience with delectable dips and salsas:

Marinara Dip: Serve your pizzadilla with a side of warm marinara sauce for a nostalgic nod to classic pizza flavors. The tangy richness of marinara complements the cheesy filling perfectly.

Creamy Avocado Salsa: Elevate your pizzadilla with a creamy avocado salsa that adds a refreshing and buttery element. This cool contrast balances the warmth and cheesiness of the pizzadilla.

Spicy Tomato Salsa: Infuse your pizzadilla experience with a touch of heat by serving it alongside a zesty tomato salsa. The combination of diced tomatoes, onions, jalapenos, and fresh cilantro adds vibrant flavors and a hint of spice.

The pizzadilla is a culinary masterpiece that brings together the best of pizza and quesadilla worlds. By mastering the layering technique, achieving crispy perfection, and pairing your pizzadillas with tantalizing dips and salsas, you'll embark on a journey of flavor fusion that delights the taste buds and expands your culinary horizons.

In the upcoming chapters, we'll continue to explore inventive twists, unique flavor combinations, and practical tips to master the art of creating perfect pepperoni pizzas.

Chapter 17: Pepperoni and Beyond: Exploring Alternative Meats

Prepare to embark on a culinary journey that ventures beyond the familiar realm of beef and pork pepperoni. In this chapter, we'll explore the fascinating world of alternative meats as pizza toppings. By stepping outside the traditional and embracing the rich flavors of lamb, the versatility of chicken, and the uniqueness of seafood, you'll elevate your pizza experience to new heights. Discover the art of marinating, the nuances of cooking techniques, and the perfect pairings that allow these non-traditional meats to shine on your pizza creations.

Lamb, Chicken, and Seafood as Pepperoni Alternatives

Experience the delightful variety that non-traditional meats bring to your pizza:

Lamb and Feta: Transport your taste buds to the Mediterranean with a lamb-infused pizza topped with crumbled feta cheese, Kalamata olives, and a sprinkle of fresh oregano. The combination evokes the flavors of Greece and creates a symphony of earthy and tangy notes.

Tandoori Chicken: Infuse your pizza with the vibrant spices of India by marinating chicken in a tandoori spice blend. The resulting flavors are warm and aromatic, pairing harmoniously with colorful bell peppers, red onion slices, and a drizzle of cooling yogurt-based sauce.

Mediterranean Seafood Medley: Elevate your pizza with a seafood extravaganza. Sautéed shrimp and tender calamari rings take center stage, while artichoke hearts, sun-dried tomatoes, and capers offer bursts of flavor. This combination echoes the freshness of coastal Mediterranean cuisine.

Marinating and Cooking Techniques for Non-Traditional Meats

Unlock the full potential of alternative meats through marinating and cooking techniques:

Lamb's Flavor Soak: Before gracing your pizza, marinate lamb in a mixture of olive oil, minced garlic, aromatic rosemary, and zesty lemon juice. This marinade not only infuses the meat with robust flavor but also tenderizes it for a succulent bite.

Chicken's Flavorful Bath: Give chicken pieces a luxurious soak in a marinade composed of creamy yogurt, tangy lemon juice, aromatic spices like cumin and coriander, and a touch of garlic. This marination ensures tender, flavorful chicken that complements a variety of toppings.

Seafood's Quick Marinade: For seafood, a brief marinade is the key. Combine zesty lemon zest, minced garlic, and a medley of fresh herbs like parsley and thyme. This quick infusion of flavor enhances the delicate taste of seafood without overwhelming it.

Exploring alternative meats as pepperoni alternatives adds depth, diversity, and a touch of adventure to your pizza creations. By embracing the flavors of lamb, the adaptability of chicken, and the unique essence of seafood, you'll unlock a world of culinary possibilities that bring out the best in your pizza toppings. The art of marinating and the finesse of cooking techniques elevate each meat to its full potential, harmonizing them with an array of flavors. Your journey beyond traditional meats enriches your pizza experience and showcases the limitless creativity that lies within the realm of alternative meat toppings.

Chapter 18: Pesto Passion: Pesto and Pepperoni Pairings

Prepare to savor the exquisite marriage of pesto's herbaceousness and pepperoni's boldness in a culinary pairing that's nothing short of exceptional. In this chapter, we'll delve into the world of pesto and pepperoni, exploring how their contrasting yet complementary flavors come together to create a taste sensation. We'll explore homemade pesto varieties tailored for pizza and guide you through the process of crafting pesto pepperoni pizzas that will leave your taste buds craving more.

The Marriage of Pesto's Herbaceous Ness and Pepperoni's Boldness

Pesto and pepperoni, seemingly unlikely partners, form a harmonious union:

Herbaceous Pesto: Pesto's fresh and herbaceous profile, often featuring basil, garlic, pine nuts, and Parmesan cheese, beautifully contrasts with the bold and slightly spicy flavors of pepperoni.

Bold Pepperoni: The robust flavors of pepperoni, with their smoky, slightly tangy, and spiced notes, create a dynamic balance when paired with the verdant and aromatic qualities of pesto.

Homemade Pesto Varieties for Pizza

Customize your pesto to enhance its compatibility with pepperoni:

Classic Basil Pesto: Craft a timeless pesto with fresh basil leaves, garlic, pine nuts, Parmesan cheese, and olive oil. Its bright and aromatic nature enhances the pepperoni's boldness.

Spinach and Walnut Pesto: Experiment with a twist by using spinach and toasted walnuts in your pesto. This variation adds earthiness and nuttiness that harmonize beautifully with pepperoni.

Sun-Dried Tomato Pesto: Elevate your pesto experience by incorporating sun-dried tomatoes, garlic, almonds, and fresh basil. The concentrated sweetness of the tomatoes complements the spiciness of pepperoni.

Classic Basil Pesto
Ingredients:

- 2 cups fresh basil leaves, packed
- 3 cloves garlic
- 1/4 cup pine nuts
- 1/2 cup grated Parmesan cheese
- 1/2 cup extra-virgin olive oil
- Salt and pepper, to taste

Instructions:

1. In a food processor, combine the basil, garlic, pine nuts, and Parmesan cheese.
2. Pulse the mixture until coarsely chopped.
3. With the food processor running, gradually add the olive oil in a steady stream until the pesto reaches your desired consistency.
4. Season with salt and pepper, and blend again to combine.
5. Taste and adjust the seasoning if needed.

Spinach and Walnut Pesto
Ingredients:

- 2 cups baby spinach leaves, packed
- 1/2 cup toasted walnuts
- 2 cloves garlic
- 1/2 cup grated Parmesan cheese
- 1/2 cup extra-virgin olive oil
- Salt and pepper, to taste

Instructions:

1. In a food processor, combine the baby spinach, toasted walnuts, garlic, and Parmesan cheese.
2. Pulse the mixture until coarsely chopped.
3. While the food processor is running, gradually add the olive oil in a steady stream until the pesto reaches a smooth consistency.
4. Season with salt and pepper, and blend again to combine.
5. Taste and adjust the seasoning as needed.

Sun-Dried Tomato Pesto

Ingredients:

- 1 cup sun-dried tomatoes (packed in oil), drained
- 1/2 cup fresh basil leaves
- 1/4 cup slivered almonds
- 2 cloves garlic
- 1/2 cup grated Parmesan cheese
- 1/4 cup extra-virgin olive oil
- Salt and pepper, to taste

Instructions:

1. In a food processor, combine the sun-dried tomatoes, fresh basil, slivered almonds, garlic, and Parmesan cheese.
2. Pulse the mixture until finely chopped.
3. While the food processor is running, gradually add the olive oil in a steady stream until the pesto becomes smooth.
4. Season with salt and pepper, and blend again to combine.
5. Taste and adjust the seasoning if necessary.

A Green and Red Delight: Pesto Pepperoni Pizzas

Unleash the potential of pesto and pepperoni by crafting flavorful pizzas:

Pesto Base: Spread a thin layer of your chosen pesto over the pizza crust, creating a vibrant and aromatic foundation for your toppings.

Pepperoni Placement: Strategically arrange pepperoni slices over the pesto, allowing their bold flavors to meld with the herbaceous Ness of the pesto.

Complementary Ingredients: Enhance the experience by adding ingredients that bridge the flavors, such as sliced black olives, roasted red bell peppers, and grated mozzarella cheese.

Baking Brilliance: Bake your pesto pepperoni pizza until the crust is golden and crispy, the cheese melts to perfection, and the aroma of the pesto and pepperoni fills the air.

Pesto passion takes on a new dimension when paired with the boldness of pepperoni. By understanding the dynamic interplay between pesto's herbaceous charm and pepperoni's robust character, and by experimenting with homemade pesto varieties tailored for pizza, you'll unlock a world of flavors that elevate your pizza creations. The green and red delight of pesto pepperoni pizzas not only tantalizes the taste buds but also invites you to explore the artistry of combining diverse ingredients for a culinary masterpiece.

Chapter 19: Cheesy Overload: Stuffed Crust Pepperoni Pizza

Prepare to take your pizza experience to a whole new level with the indulgent delight of stuffed crust pepperoni pizza. In this chapter, we'll embark on a cheesy adventure, exploring the art of creating a crust that's not only crisp and flavorful but also hides a luscious pocket of melted cheese. Discover the joy of stretching and pulling gooey cheese, and explore the possibilities of different stuffing options that will satisfy your cravings for the ultimate cheese experience.

The Ultimate Cheesy Indulgence: Stuffed Crust

Stuffed crust pizza is a symphony of textures and flavors that transforms each bite into an experience of pure indulgence:

Surprise Inside: The magic of stuffed crust lies in the unexpected layer of melted cheese hidden within the crust. As you bite into your pizza, you'll be greeted by a luxurious burst of creamy richness.

Texture Play: Stuffed crust introduces a delightful contrast of textures – the initial crunch of the outer crust followed by the sumptuous stretch of melted cheese. It's a sensory delight that elevates your pizza enjoyment.

Stuffing Options: From Classic Cheese to Creative Fillings

Customize your stuffed crust experience by experimenting with various stuffing options:

Classic Mozzarella: Embrace the timeless joy of a stuffed crust by using mozzarella cheese. Its mild flavor and exceptional meltability create the ultimate cheese pull experience that everyone loves.

Three-Cheese Blend: Elevate the complexity of flavors by opting for a three-cheese blend as your stuffing. The combination of mozzarella, cheddar, and Parmesan brings layers of richness and depth.

Spinach and Ricotta: Embark on a gourmet journey by incorporating sautéed spinach and creamy ricotta cheese. This stuffing option introduces a touch of elegance and a harmonious balance of flavors.

Achieving the Perfect Stretchy Cheese Pull

Master the art of creating the iconic cheese pull that's synonymous with stuffed crust pizza:

Even Distribution: Ensure that your cheese stuffing is distributed uniformly along the inner edge of the pizza crust. This guarantees that every slice boasts the same gooey cheese goodness.

Seal with Care: Press the edges of the crust together firmly to seal in the cheese stuffing, preventing any leakage during the baking process.

Baking Precision: Follow the recommended baking temperature and duration to allow the cheese inside the crust to melt to perfection. The result should be a pocket of molten cheese waiting to be discovered.

Pulling Technique: When you're ready to enjoy your stuffed crust slice, gently pull the stuffed edge away from the rest of the pizza. Watch in awe as the cheese stretches in all its glory.

Stuffed crust pepperoni pizza isn't just a dish; it's an experience that celebrates the joy of indulgence and innovation. By mastering the art of creating a perfect stuffed crust, experimenting with different stuffing options, and achieving the captivating cheese pull, you'll embark on a journey that showcases the incredible possibilities within the world of pizza. The cheesy overload of stuffed crust pepperoni pizza is an ode to the sheer pleasure of pushing culinary boundaries.

Chapter 20: Sweet Finale: Dessert Pizza with a Pepperoni Twist

Prepare to indulge your sweet tooth and unleash your creativity as we venture into the realm of dessert pizzas with a unique pepperoni twist. In this chapter, we'll reimagine the concept of pizza as a canvas for sweet flavors, where the rich and savory essence of pepperoni adds an unexpected yet delightful element. Explore the art of crafting dessert pizzas that bridge the gap between sweet and savory, offering a crowd-pleasing finale to your culinary journey.

Sugary Satisfaction: Dessert Pizzas Reimagined

Discover the exciting transformation of pizza into a dessert masterpiece:

Unexpected Dessert: Rethink the traditional notions of pizza by exploring dessert versions that embrace sugary satisfaction and offer a delightful departure from savory flavors.

Creative Canvas: Dessert pizzas provide a unique canvas for culinary innovation, where you can experiment with various sweet toppings and combinations.

Incorporating Sweet and Savory with Pepperoni

Elevate your dessert pizza experience by adding a pepperoni twist:

Unexpected Harmony: The addition of pepperoni introduces a savory component that balances the sweetness of dessert pizzas. The interplay of flavors creates a dynamic and unexpected harmony.

Umami Boost: Pepperoni's umami-rich profile enhances the overall depth of flavor, adding complexity to the dessert's taste profile.

Crowd-Pleasing Dessert Pizzas for Special Occasions

Craft dessert pizzas that steal the show at special occasions:

Nutella and Banana Delight: Spread a layer of Nutella on the pizza crust, top it with sliced bananas, and sprinkle crumbled pepperoni for an alluring blend of sweet and savory.

Berries and Mascarpone: Create a dessert masterpiece by layering mascarpone cheese, fresh berries, and a drizzle of honey. The addition of pepperoni provides a surprising burst of flavor.

Caramel Apple Extravaganza: Transform your dessert pizza with caramelized apple slices, a drizzle of caramel sauce, and a scattering of chopped pepperoni for a taste of autumn indulgence.

The sweet finale of dessert pizzas with a pepperoni twist is a testament to the endless possibilities of culinary creativity. By combining unexpected flavors, experimenting with sweet and savory contrasts, and crafting crowd-pleasing dessert pizzas, you'll leave a lasting impression on your taste buds and those of your guests. The pepperoni twist serves as a reminder that innovation knows no bounds, even within the realm of dessert.

As we conclude our exploration of pepperoni pizza in its many forms, I hope you're inspired to continue experimenting, creating, and sharing your culinary passion with others. Whether it's a classic pepperoni slice, an inventive gourmet creation, or a sweet surprise, the world of pepperoni pizza invites you to savor every bite and embrace the joy of culinary discovery.